COMBINED PERCUSSION

LEVEL 1

BELWIN 21st Century Band Method

by JACK BULLOCK and ANTHONY MAIELLO

Congratulations on choosing to play a musical instrument. You will have many hours and many years of fun playing and performing in the band. This book has everything you need to learn to play. If you would like to know more, there is a video just for your instrument. You can play along at home with the CD accompaniments, with SmartMusic Studio™ or with the video—just as if you were in the band! You now belong to a special group of people around the world—people who love to make music, now and into the 21st Century!

WELCOME TO THE BAND!

from all of us at Alfred Publishing

Jack Bullock and Anthony Maiello

In this Combined Percussion book, the Snare Drum, Bass Drum, and Auxiliary Percussion parts are on the left-hand pages. The Keyboard Percussion parts are on the right-hand pages (the "A" pages).

Editor: Thom Proctor
Production Coordinator: Edmond Randle
Cover Photo: Roberto Santos
Technical Editor: Dale Sloman
Finale Engraver: Rosario Ortiz
Art Design: Joseph Klucar
Art Coordinator: Thais Yanes

Percussion on cover courtesy of LUDWIG INDUSTRIES,
A DIVISION OF THE SELMER COMPANY, INC..

DRUMS AND AUXILIARY PERCUSSION

PRACTICE MAKES BETTER:

Make time to practice every day. Pick a place where you will have good light and good air circulation, and where you will not be bothered. You should have plenty of room for a good chair and your music stand so you keep good position and posture. Keep track of how many minutes you practice. Work hard and have fun playing!

Week	Date	LESSON ASSIGNMENT	Sun.	Mon.	Tues.	Wed.	Thurs.	Fri.	Sat.	Total
1										
2										
3										
4										
5										
6										
7										
8										
9										
10										
11										
12										
13										
14										
15										
16										
17										
18										
19										
20										
21										
22										
23										
24										
25										
26										
27										
28										
29										
30										
31										
32										
33										
34										
35										
36										

Practice can be even better and more fun if you play along with the CD accompaniments, with Smart Music Studio™ accompaniments or with the video for your instrument. Ask your teacaher or at your music store for more information on these products.

KEYBOARD PERCUSSION

PRACTICE MAKES BETTER:

Make time to practice every day. Pick a place where you will have good light and good air circulation, and where you will not be bothered. You should have plenty of room for a good chair and your music stand so you keep good position and posture. Keep track of how many minutes you practice. Work hard and have fun playing!

Week	Date	LESSON ASSIGNMENT	Sun.	Mon.	Tues.	Wed.	Thurs.	Fri.	Sat.	Total
1										
2										
3										
4										
5										
6										
7										
8										
9										
10										
11										
12										
13										
14										
15										
16										
17										
18										
19										
20										
21										
22										
23										
24										
25										
26										
27										
28										
29										
30										
31										
32										
33										
34										
35										
36										

Practice can be even better and more fun if you play along with the CD accompaniments, with Smart Music Studio™ accompaniments or with the video for your instrument. Ask your teacaher or at your music store for more information on these products.

GET READY TO PLAY
DRUMS AND AUXILIARY PERCUSSION

STAFF

A Staff has five lines and four spaces.

CLEF SIGN

A clef sign is a symbol placed on the staff.

A B C D E F G A B C D E F G

The first seven letters of the alphabet
are used in music to name the lines and spaces.

Names of the Lines and Spaces.
(For keyboard percussion instruments)

BAR LINE AND MEASURE

bar lines

measure

A bar line is a line drawn through the staff.
A measure is the distance between two bar lines.

FINAL BAR LINE

A final bar line has a thin bar line
and a thick bar line which indicates the end.

TIME SIGNATURE

There are four counts in four/four time.

A time signature is placed at the beginning of the
staff and indicates the number of counts in a measure.

NOTE

Note heads   stem   flag

The parts of a note.

ACCIDENTALS

Flats, Sharps, and Naturals are called accidentals.

Whole Note

Receives four counts of sound in 4/4 time.

Whole Rest

Receives four counts of silence in 4/4 time.

3

GET READY TO PLAY
KEYBOARD PERCUSSION

STAFF

A Staff has five lines and four spaces.

CLEF SIGN

A clef sign is a symbol placed on the staff.

A B C D E F G A B C D E F G

The first seven letters of the alphabet
are used in music to name the lines and spaces.

Names of the Lines and Spaces.

BAR LINE AND MEASURE

bar lines

measure

A bar line is a line drawn through the staff.
A measure is the distance between two bar lines.

FINAL BAR LINE

A final bar line has a thin bar line
and a thick bar line which indicates the end.

TIME SIGNATURE

There are four counts in four/four time.

A time signature is placed at the beginning of the
staff and indicates the number of counts in a measure.

NOTE

Note heads   stem   flag

The parts of a note.

ACCIDENTALS

Flats, Sharps, and Naturals are called accidentals.

Whole Note

Receives four counts of sound in 4/4 time.

Whole Rest

Receives four counts of silence in 4/4 time.

Lesson 1

Percussion

Quarter Note

Receives one count in 4/4 time.

Quarter Rest

Receives one count in 4/4 time.

R = Right Hand
L = Left Hand

Alternate Strokes

R L R L R L, etc.
L R L R L R, etc

1.

2.

3.

4. Groovin' 'N' Moovin'

5. Hand Off
Are you counting?

6. The Seesaw
Count!

7. Easy Does It
Count!

8. Balloon Ride
Count!

Extra Credit Exercise 1
See page 30 and 31

9. Write The Beats   Write the counting for each measure, then play.

Lesson 2

Percussion

Half Note

Receives two counts in 4/4 time

Half Rest

Receives two counts in 4/4 time

Double Strokes

R R L L

Duet

A piece for two performers to play together

1.

Counting: 1 2 3 4 1 2 3 4 1 2 3 4 1 2 3 4 1 2 3 4 1 2 3 4

2.

Counting: 1 2 3 4 1 2 3 4 1 2 3 4 1 2 3 4 1 2 3 4 1 2 3 4

3. Half Note Trip

Counting: 1 2 3 4 1 2 3 4 1 2 3 4 1 2 3 4 1 2 3 4 1 2 3 4

4. Jive With Five

Counting: 1 2 3 4 1 2 3 4 1 2 3 4 1 2 3 4 1 2 3 4 1 2 3 4

5. Hot Cross Buns

Traditional, U.S.A.

Are you counting?

6. Dippin' Down

7. At Pierrot's Door

Alternate Strokes

French Folk Song

8. Tune For Two

(Duet)

Alternate Strokes

Practice 8 and then 9. Then play 8 and 9 together as a duet.

9.

Alternate Strokes

5

Lesson 3

Percussion

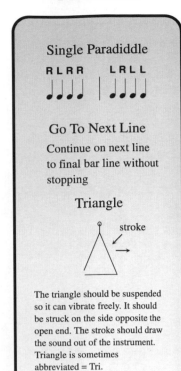

Single Paradiddle

RLRR   LRLL
♩♩♩♩ | ♩♩♩♩

Go To Next Line

Continue on next line to final bar line without stopping

Triangle

stroke

The triangle should be suspended so it can vibrate freely. It should be struck on the side opposite the open end. The stroke should draw the sound out of the instrument. Triangle is sometimes abbreviated = Tri.

1.

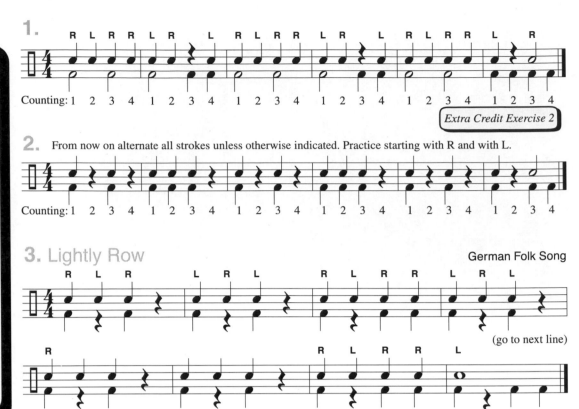

Counting: 1 2 3 4 1 2 3 4 1 2 3 4 1 2 3 4 1 2 3 4 1 2 3 4

Extra Credit Exercise 2

2. From now on alternate all strokes unless otherwise indicated. Practice starting with R and with L.

Counting: 1 2 3 4 1 2 3 4 1 2 3 4 1 2 3 4 1 2 3 4 1 2 3 4

3. Lightly Row

German Folk Song

(go to next line)

4. Lullaby

Triangle

Kashmiri Folk Song

5. Dodo, L'Enfant Dors
(Sleep, Baby Sleep)

Triangle

Belgian Folk Song

6. Some Folks
(Duet)

Practice each separately, then play 6 and 7 as a duet.

Stephen Collins Foster, U.S.A.

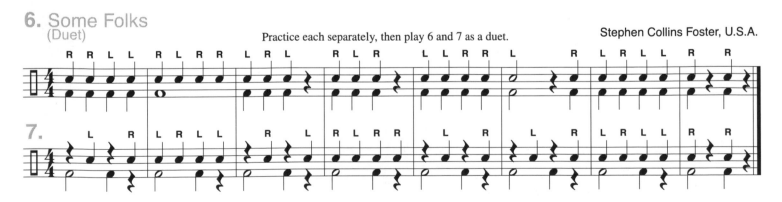

7.

8. Draw a clef sign and a time signature. Then draw the bar lines. Write the counting beneath the line and then play the rhythm.

6

Keyboard Percussion

Quarter Note

Receives one count
in 4/4 time

Quarter Rest

Receives one count
in 4/4 time

Go To Next Line

Continue on next line
to final bar line without
stopping

1.

Counting: 1 2 3 4   1 2 3 4   1 2 3 4   1 2 3 4   1 2 3 4   1 2 3 4

2.

Counting: 1 2 3 4   1 2 3 4   1 2 3 4   1 2 3 4   1 2 3 4   1 2 3 4

3. Lightly Row

German Folk Song

(go to next line)

4. Lullaby

Kashmiri Folk Song

5. Dodo, L'Enfant Dors
(Sleep, Baby Sleep)

Belgian Folk Song

Extra Credit Exercise 2

6. Some Folks
(Duet)

Practice each separately, then play 6 and 7 as a duet.

Stephen Collins Foster, U.S.A.

7.

8. Draw a clef sign and a time signature. Then draw the bar lines. Write the counting beneath the line and then play.

Lesson 4

Percussion

Stick on Rim

Strike the rim with the middle of the stick.

Repeat sign

Go back to the beginning and repeat

2/4 Time Signature

2 - two counts in each measure
4 - a quarter note receives one count

1.

2. New Note Rock

3. Rocket Ride

4. Scaling Up And Down

5. Chorale (Duet)

Triangle

Practice 5 and 6 separately, then play as a duet.

6.

7. Tzena, Tzena, Tzena, Tzena (Rock)

R.H. on rim   L.H. on drum

Israeli Folk Song

Extra Credit Exercise 3

8. Percussion Workout

Start slowly and gradually get faster.

7

Songs For The Fun Of It

Percussion

Jingle Bells

James Pierpont, U.S.A.

Love Somebody

Traditional

¿Que Pasa?

(What's Up?)

Rockin' With Mr(s). "T"

(Substitute the initial of your teacher)

R.H. on rim   L.H. on drum

Songs For The Fun Of It

Keyboard Percussion

Jingle Bells

James Pierpont, U.S.A.

Love Somebody

Traditional

¿Que Pasa?
(What's Up?)

Rockin' With Mr(s). "T"
(Substitute the initial of your teacher)

Our First Concert

Percussion

Alpha March

Jack Bullock, U.S.A.

Arroro Mi Niño

Argentine Folk Song

Jolly Old St. Nicholas

Traditional

The Saints Go Marching In

James M. Black and
Katherine E. Purvis, U.S.A.

Our First Concert

Keyboard Percussion

Alpha March

Jack Bullock, U.S.A.

Arroro Mi Niño

Argentine Folk Song

Jolly Old St. Nicholas

Traditional

The Saints Go Marching In

James M. Black and
Katherine E. Purvis, U.S.A.

Lesson 5

Percussion

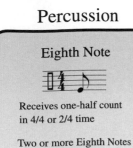

Eighth Note

Receives one-half count
in 4/4 or 2/4 time

Two or more Eighth Notes

Are connected by a beam

Flam

Snares off: Use snare strainer
to release snares from the
bottom head.

1. Tricky Mickey

2. Twinkle, Twinkle Little Star

France, England

Rim and/or Tri.

3. Down Under

4. Skip To My Lou

Traditional, U.S.A.

5. Ten Little Maidens

Traditional

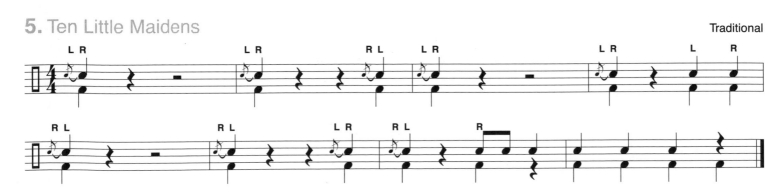

6. Quail Song

Cherokee Indian

Snares off

Extra Credit Exercise 4

1. Tricky Mickey

same

1 + 2 + 1 2   1 + 2 + 1 2   1 + 2 + 1 2

2. Twinkle, Twinkle Little Star

France, England

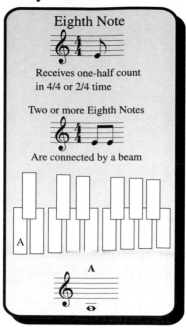

Eighth Note

Receives one-half count in 4/4 or 2/4 time

Two or more Eighth Notes

Are connected by a beam

A

3. Down Under

4. Skip To My Lou

Traditional, U.S.A.

5. Ten Little Maidens

Traditional

6. Quail Song

Cherokee Indian

Extra Credit Exercise 4

Lesson 6

Percussion

Tie

The curved line is a tie that connects two notes of the same pitch. Strike the first note only.

Suspended Cymbal

The suspended cymbal should be played with a snare drum stick or yarn mallet. Sometimes the abbreviation is Susp. Cym.

Round

A melody played by two or more performers starting at different times.

1. All Tied Up

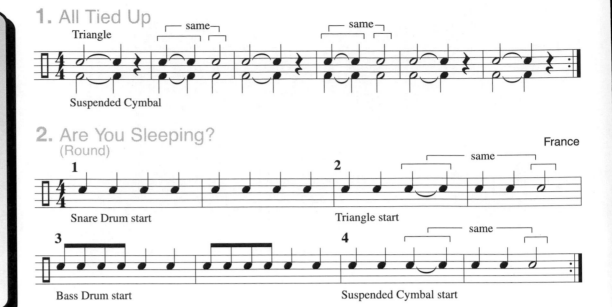

2. Are You Sleeping?
(Round)

France

3. The Bridge Of Avignon

French Folk Song

4. Up On The Housetop
(Duet)

Benjamin Russel Hanby, U.S.A.

Practice each part, then play 4/4a and 5/5a as a duet.

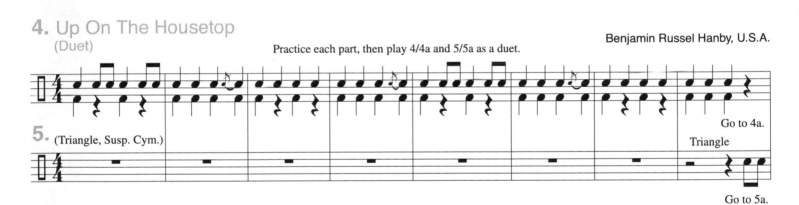

5. (Triangle, Susp. Cym.)

Go to 4a.

Triangle

Go to 5a.

4a.

Snares off

5a.

Susp. Cym.

6. Percussion Workout

11

Lesson 6

1. All Tied Up

2. Are You Sleeping?
(Round)

Keyboard Percussion

Tie

The curved line is a tie that connects two notes of the same pitch. Strike the first note only.

Round

A melody played by two or more performers starting at different times.

3. The Bridge Of Avignon

French Folk Song

4. Up On The Housetop
(Duet)

Practice each part, then play 4/4a and 5/5a as a duet.

Benjamin Russel Hanby, U.S.A.

5.

Go to 4a.

Go to 5a.

4a.

5a.

6. Finger Workout

11A

Lesson 7

Percussion

3/4 Time Signature
3 - Three counts in each measure
4 - A quarter note receives one count

Flam Accent

Dot
♩. = ♩♪
1 2 3   1 2 3

The Dot following a note is equal to one-half the value of that note.

1. Chiapanecas
Flam Accent
Mexican Folk Song

2. A Jazzy Threesome
Triangle
same
Suspended Cymbal   1   2   3   1   2   3

3. Beautiful Brown Eyes
American Folk Song

4. Long, Long Ago
Thomas Haynes Bayly, England

5. The Donkey
(Round)
Traditional

Snare Drum and Bass Drum start   Triangle start   Suspended Cymbal start

Extra Credit Exercise 5

6.
_____ (Title)   _____ (Title)   Your name

Compose your own rhythms and then play each.

12

Lesson 8

Percussion

Flam Tap

LR R RL L

1st and 2nd endings

| 1. | | 2. |

Play the first ending the first time and the second ending the second time.

1.

2. Yankee Doodle

Flam Tap

American Folk Song

LR R RL L   LR R RL L   LR R RL L   LR   RL

LR R RL L   LR R RL L   LR R RL L   LR   RL

3. The Mocking Bird

American Folk Song

4. Barcarole

Triangle and Suspended Cymbal

Jacques Offenbach, France

| 1. Play 1st time only | 2. Play 2nd time only |

second time

5. Down In The Valley

American Folk Song

| 1. | 2. |

6. Just Rockin' 'N' Rollin'
(Duet)

R.H. on Rim   L.H. on Drum

Practice each separately, then play as a duet.

7. Suspended Cymbal

Extra Credit Exercise 6

Lesson 9

Percussion

Triangle and Susp. Cym. may also be notated on the top space as:

Pickup Note(s)

Note(s) in an incomplete measure before the first bar line.

Forward Repeat Sign:

Point of return (in place of the beginning) for repeated section

Wood Block

Play with a stick or rubber mallet. Sometimes it is abbreviated W.B.

1. Check It Out

S.D. and Triangle

B.D.

2. Russian Folk Dance

Ludwig van Beethoven, Germany

L.H. on head   R.H. on rim

3. Blue Moon

Music by Richard Rodgers
Lyrics by Lorenz Hart, U.S.A.

Suspended Cymbal and Rim
Pick up note

© 1934 (Renewed 1962) EMI ROBBINS CATALOG INC.
and WARNER BROS. PUBLICATIONS U.S. INC.

4. Buenos Días Su Señoría
(Good Day, Your Highness)

Chilean Folk Song

Pick up notes

5. Polly Wolly Doodle

Snare Drum and Wood Block

Traditional, U.S.A.

6. Carousel
(A Merry-Go-"Round")

Triangle start

Snare Drum start

Suspended Cymbal start

7. Percussion Workout

Lesson 9

Keyboard Percussion

1. Check It Out

2. Russian Folk Dance

Ludwig van Beethoven, Germany

3. Blue Moon

Music by Richard Rodgers
Lyrico by Loronz Hart, U.S.A.

Pick up note

4   1 2 3 4 1

1 2 3

© 1934 (Renewed 1962) EMI ROBBINS CATALOG INC.
and WARNER BROS. PUBLICATIONS U.S. INC.

Key Signature

The flats or sharps before the time signature which indicates the key center (Do)

Key of B♭ (Do = B♭)

There are two flats in the Key of B♭

Pickup Note(s)

Note(s) in an incomplete measure before the first bar line.

Forward Repeat Sign:

Point of return (in place of the beginning) for repeated section

4. Buenos Días Su Señoría
(Good Day, Your Highness)

Chilean Folk Song

Pick up notes

3 4   1

1   2

5. Polly Wolly Doodle

Traditional, U.S.A.

4 + 1

6. Carousel
(A Merry-Go-"Round")

1   2

3

7. Keyboard Percussion Workout

14A

Lesson 10

Percussion

Eighth Rests

Receives one-half count in 4/4, 2/4 and 3/4 times

1. Sound Familiar?

2. English Melody

England

3. Foggy Dew

England

4. Keep 'Em Even

Extra Credit Exercise 7

5. Bingo

American Folk Song

6. Pickup Twister

Write the counting, clap the rhythms as you count out loud, then play.

a. **b.** **c.** **d.**

1. Sound Familiar?

Keyboard Percussion

2. English Melody

Always look at the key signature before playing

England

3. Foggy Dew

England

Key Signature
Key of E♭

All B's are lowered to B flat (B♭); all E's are lowered to E flat (E♭); and all A's are lowered to A flat (A♭).

Eighth Rests

Receives one-half count in 4/4, 2/4 and 3/4 times

4. Keep 'Em Even

1 + 2 + 1 + 2 +

Extra Credit Exercise 7

5. Bingo

American Folk Song

6. Pickup Twister

Write the counting, clap the rhythms as you count out loud, then play.

a.   b.   c.   d.

More Songs Just For The Fun Of It

Percussion

This Old Man

Wood Block

American Folk Song

Tell Me Why

Triangle

Traditional

Theme From Symphony № 1

Snares off

Johannes Brahms, Germany

1.

2.

Rockin' Old Mac

Rim and/or Suspended Cymbal

Erskine MacDonald, England

This Land Is Your Land

(rim)

R

Woody Guthrie, U.S.A.

16

More Songs Just For The Fun Of It

Keyboard Percussion

This Old Man

American Folk Song

Tell Me Why

Traditional

Theme From Symphony № 1

Johannes Brahms, Germany

Rockin' Old Mac

Erskine MacDonald, England

This Land Is Your Land

Woody Guthrie, U.S.A.

Concert Time Nº 2

Percussion

Theme From The Surprise Symphony

Joseph Haydn, Austria

Aura Lee

William Whiteman Fosdick
and George R. Poulton, U.S.A.

The Carnival Of Venice

Italian Folk Song

Folk Dance

Béla Bártok, Hungary

Concert Time Nº 2

Keyboard Percussion

Theme From The Surprise Symphony

Joseph Haydn, Austria

Aura Lee

William Whiteman Fosdick
and George R. Poulton, U.S.A.

The Carnival Of Venice

Italian Folk Song

Folk Dance

Béla Bártok, Hungary

17A

Lesson 11

Percussion

Dotted quarter and eighth rhythm

1 + 2 +

Tempo

The speed of the music.
(Slow, Quick)

Ritard. - gradually slower

Sixteenth Notes

1 + 2 +

1 e + a 2 e + a

1.

2. Crazy Fingers

Slow

3. Hold It!

Slow ——— same ———

Extra Credit Exercise 8

4. America

Quick

Always check your music for the instruments you will need to play.

Samuel Francis Smith, U.S.A.
Triangle

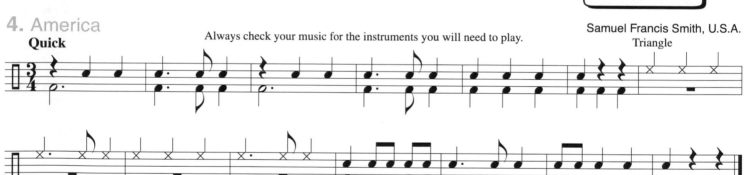

ritard.

5. Ecossaise

Quick   Suspended Cymbal

Ludwig van Beethoven, Germany

6. Percussion Workout

1 e + a 2 + 3 e + a 4 +

Extra Credit Exercise 9

Lesson 11

Keyboard Percussion

1.

2. Crazy Fingers

3. Hold It!

Extra Credit Exercise 8

4. America

Samuel Francis Smith, U.S.A.

ritard.

5. Ecossaise

Ludwig van Beethoven, Germany

6. Keyboard Percussion Workout

A B♭ C D E♭ F G A

Extra Credit Exercise 9

A♭

Dotted quarter and
eighth rhythm

1 + 2 +

Tempo

The speed of the music.
(Slow, Quick)

Ritard. - gradually slower

18A

Lesson 12

Percussion

Eighth and Sixteenth Notes

Tempo

Andante - Italian word for slow
Allegro - Italian word for fast

1. An Accidental Encounter

2. Now Is The Month Of Maying

Andante

England

Tri. and Susp. Cym.

ritard.

2a. Percussion Workout

Percussion music is sometimes written on a single line staff.

1 e + a 2 e +   1 e + a 2 + a   1 + a 2 + a   1 e + 2

3. The Sad Clown

Andante

1.   2.

4. Watch Out!

Allegro

Wood Block

5. A Little Dance

Allegro

Extra Credit Exercise 10

Dmitri Kabalevsky, Russia

6. Sunrise, Sunset

Andante Snares off

Lyrics by Sheldon Harnick
Music by Jerry Bock, U.S.A.

ritard.

Lesson 13

Percussion

Tacet = Don't play

Rolls

A Roll is indicated by the slashes on the note stem.

5 Stroke Roll

RRLLR

Triangle Rolls are played by rapidly alternating the beater from side to side in a closed corner of the triangle.

Suspended Cymbal Rolls are played by rapidly alternating strokes.

Dynamics

The loud and soft sounds in music

Soft - play quietly

Loud - play loudly

1. Careful! Don't Break It! (Tacet)

1a. 5 Stroke Roll Workout   Gradually play faster.

2. Slur It
(Duet)   Practice each exercise, then play together.

Andante

3. Susp. Cym. and/or Triangle

Extra Credit Exercise 11

4. The Old Oaken Bucket
(Duet)   Practice each exercise, then play together.   Samuel Woodworth, U.S.A.

Allegro

5. Soft   Wood Block

Soft

6. The Yankee Doodle Boy

George M. Cohan, U.S.A.

Allegro

Loud

20

1. Careful! Don't Break It! (Tacet)

1a. Keyboard Percussion Roll Workout

Keyboard Percussion

Tacet - Don't play

Roll - Rapidly alternate strokes to produce a smooth, sustained sound.

A roll is indicated by the slashes on the note stem

Slur

A curved line connecting two notes of *different* pitches. Roll the first note only.

Dynamics

The loud and soft sounds in music
Soft - play quietly
Loud - play loudly

2. Slur It

(Duet)   Practice each exercise, then play together.

Extra Credit Exercise 11

4. The Old Oaken Bucket

(Duet)   Practice each exercise, then play together.   Samuel Woodworth, U.S.A.

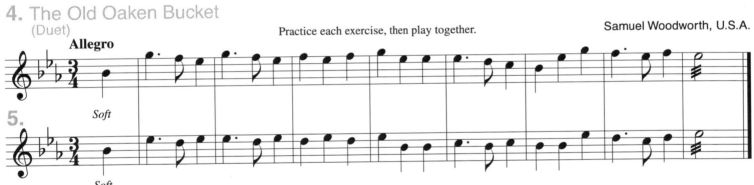

6. The Yankee Doodle Boy

George M. Cohan, U.S.A.

Lesson 14

Percussion

1. A Warmup Exercise

Andante

Triangle and Suspended Cymbal

2. Slip, Slide and Slur

Moderato

Alternate Strokes

RRLLRRLLR LLRRLLRRL

Extra Credit Exercise 12

3. Erie Canal
(Duet)

Moderato

Samuel Woodworth, U.S.A.

S.D., W.B.

Practice each exercise, then play together.

B.D.

4.

Triangle

ritard.

5. The Trolley Song

Moderato

Music by Ralph Blane
Lyrics by Hugh Martin, U.S.A.

(rim)

6. Percussion Workout

Andante

Play four times.

1. A Warmup Exercise

Andante

2. Slip, Slide and Slur

Moderato

Extra Credit Exercise 12

3. Erie Canal
(Duet)

Samuel Woodworth, U.S.A.

Practice each exercise, then play together.

Moderato

4.

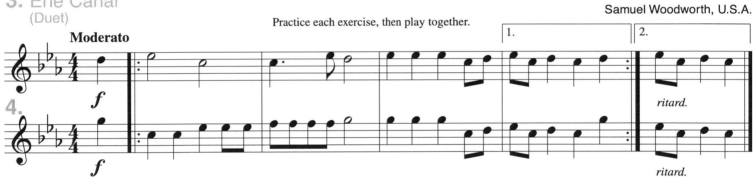

5. The Trolley Song

Music by Ralph Blane
Lyrics by Hugh Martin, U.S.A.

Moderato

6. Keyboard Percussion Workout

Andante

slurs can be above or below notes

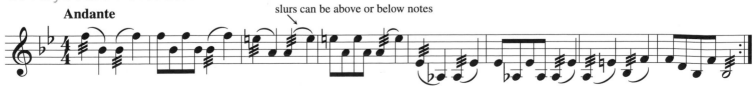

Lesson 15

Percussion

Dynamics

gradually get louder

gradually get softer

mp = **Moderately soft**

mf = **Moderately loud**

rit. = *ritard.*

Afterbeats - notes which occur on the second half of the beat

1. Rim. and/or Susp. Cym.

2. On Parade
Moderato

3. Chorale
Andante
Susp. Cym. w/Mallets

4. After Beats
Moderato

5. More After Beats

6. A Russian Polka
(Duet)

Extra Credit Exercise 13

Practice each exercise, then play together.

Allegro

7. W.B.

8. Rock It To Me
Allegro Rim and/or Susp. Cym.

Lesson 16

Percussion

Fermata

Hold the note longer than note value

Roll using double strokes.

Eighth and dotted quarter rhythm

1 + 2 + 1 + 2 +

1. Etude

Moderato

Carl Czerny, Austria

Triangle

S.D.

B.D.

2. Switcharoo

Andante

same

1 + 2 + 3 + 4 + 1 + 2 + 3 + 4

Extra Credit Exercise 14

3. Camptown Races

Moderato

Stephen Collins Foster, U.S.A.

rit.

4. Can You Name This Song?
(Duet)

Moderato

Practice each exercise, then play together.

Traditional

Rim

5. Tri.

W.B.

Lesson 17

Percussion

Remember:

To play a rest on the Triangle or Suspended Cymbal you must stop the instrument from vibrating (ringing). This technique is called damping. Grasp the instrument with the fingertips to stop the sound.

1.
Andante
Susp. Cym. or Triangle

2. A Scale Etude

Extra Credit Exercise 15

3. Hungarian Rhapsody № 14
Andante
Wood Block

Franz Liszt, Hungary

4. Bugler's Holiday
Allegro

Leroy Anderson, U.S.A.

© 1954 (Renewed 1982) EMI MILLS MUSIC, INC.

5. Be A Composer

Complete this rhythm by adding eighth notes or eighth rests. Then play.

Keyboard Percussion

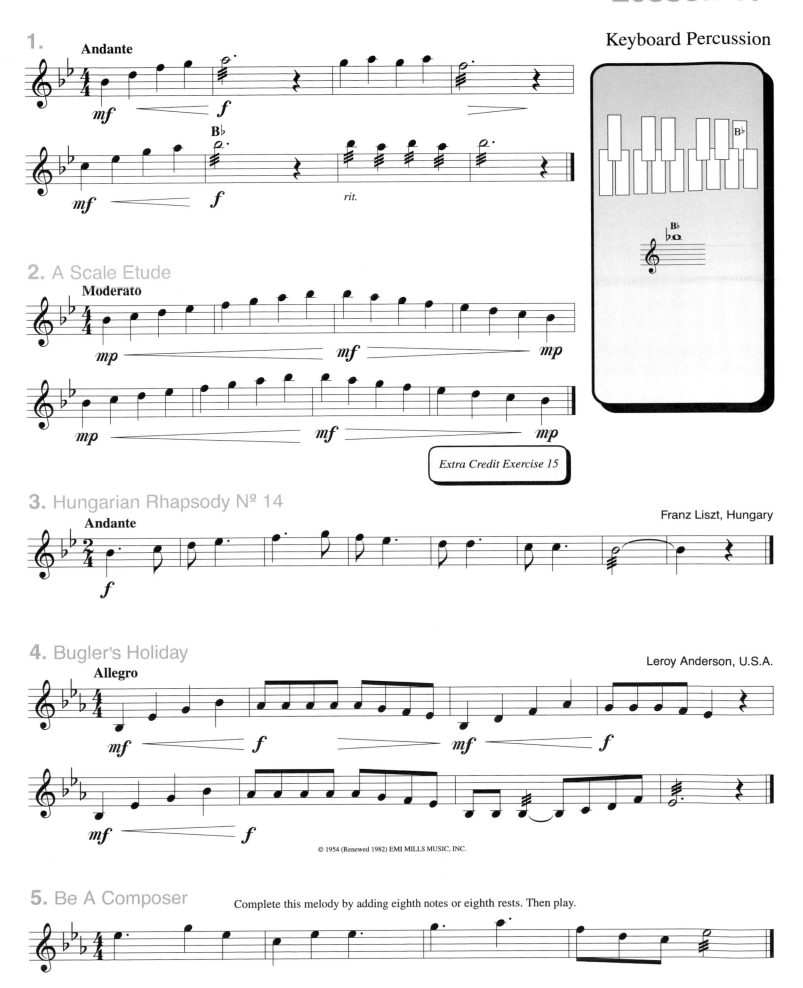

1.
Andante

2. A Scale Etude
Moderato

Extra Credit Exercise 15

3. Hungarian Rhapsody № 14

Franz Liszt, Hungary

Andante

4. Bugler's Holiday

Leroy Anderson, U.S.A.

Allegro

5. Be A Composer   Complete this melody by adding eighth notes or eighth rests. Then play.

Lesson 18

Percussion

Multiple Bounce Roll

When a smooth sustained sound is desired, a roll can be played with multiple bounces on each hand rather than using double strokes. Let each stroke "buzz" three or more times on the drum head.

Multiple measures rest

2

Rest the amount of measures shown by the number.

1. Andante

Extra Credit Exercise 16

1a. Snare Drum Workout

2. Andante

Multiple Bounce Roll

3. Siranda
(Duet)
Moderato

Practice each exercise, then play together.

Portuguese Folk Song

4. W.B.

5. Hop, Hop, Hop
(Duet)
Allegro

Practice 5 and 6, then play together.

German Folk Song

6. Susp. Cym. and/or Triangle

Count: 1   2   2   2

Keyboard Percussion

1. Andante
mp ——— *f* ——— *mf*

Extra Credit Exercise 16

2. Andante
mf ——— *f* ——— *mf* ——— *f*
mf ——— *mp*

Multiple measures rest

2 =

Rest the amount of measures shown by the number.

3. Siranda
(Duet)
Practice each exercise, then play together.
Portuguese Folk Song
Moderato
mf
rit.

4.
mf
rit.

5. Hop, Hop, Hop
(Duet)
Practice 5 and 6, then play together.
German Folk Song
Allegro
f

6.
f
Count: 1   2   2   2

2
Count: 1   2   2   2
mf ——— *f*
mf ——— *f*

25A

Still More Fun Songs

Amazing Grace

Marine's Hymn

Danny Boy

Still More Fun Songs

Keyboard Percussion

Amazing Grace

Traditional

Andante

mp

mf

mp

Marine's Hymn

Traditional, U.S.A.

Allegro

mf   f

1.

mf

2.

mf

f

Danny Boy

Frederick E. Weatherly, England

Andante

mp   mf   mp

mf   mp   mf

mp

The Sidewalks Of New York
(East Side, West Side)

Percussion

Charles B. Lawlor
and James W. Blake, U.S.A.

La Bamba

Mexico

The Sidewalks Of New York

(East Side, West Side)

Keyboard Percussion

Charles B. Lawlor
and James W. Blake, U.S.A.

Moderato

La Bamba

Moderato

Mexico

CHORALE AND VARIANTS

CHORALE AND VARIANTS

Keyboard Percussion

ROBERT WASHBURN (ASCAP)

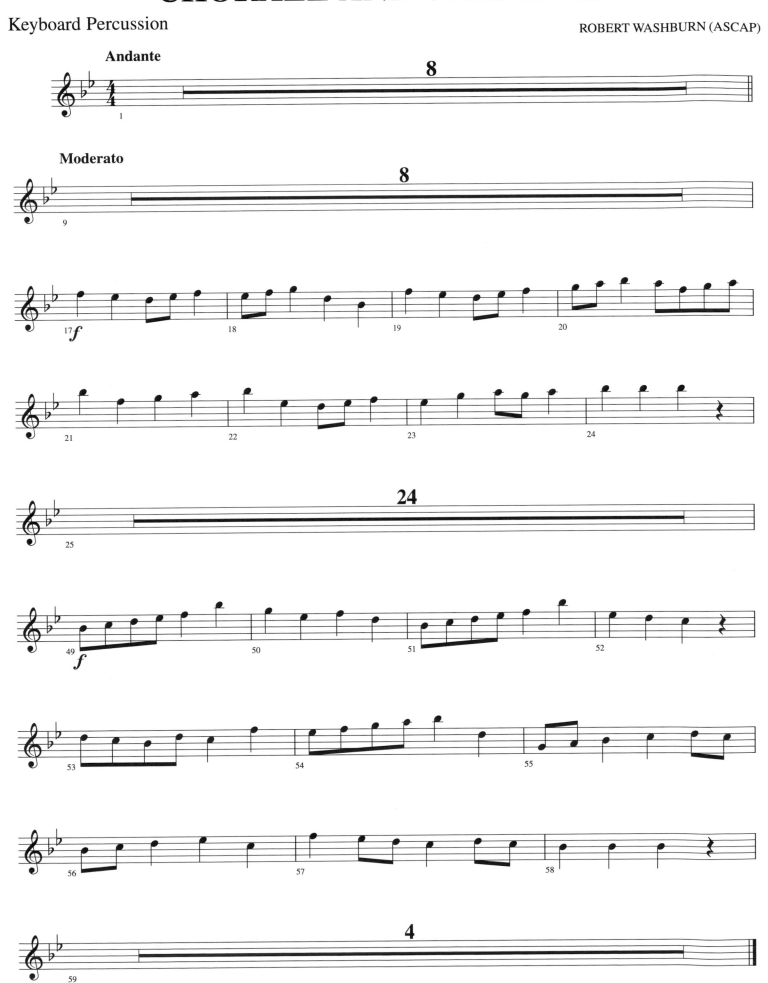

COMMENCEMENT

(An Overture for Band)

Percussion

ROBERT W. SMITH

COMMENCEMENT
(An Overture for Band)

Keyboard Percussion

ROBERT W. SMITH

Extra Credit Exercises

Percussion

1. | *Use after lesson 1, line 8*

2. | *Use after lesson 3, line 1*

R L R R L R L L R L R L R L R L R R L R L R L R L L

3. | *Use after lesson 4, line 7*

Triangle and/or Rim

4. | *Use after lesson 5, line 6*

Snares off   Snares on

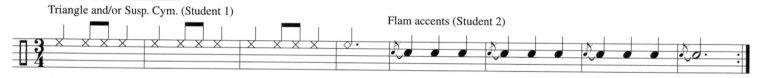

5. | *Use after lesson 7, line 5*

Triangle and/or Susp. Cym. (Student 1)   Flam accents (Student 2)

6. | *Use after lesson 8, line 7*

R.H. Rim, L.H. Drum

Flam taps

7. | *Use after lesson 10, line 4*

Play the rhythm on all instruments: Snare Drum, Bass Drum, Suspended Cymbal, Triangle, Wood Block.

8. | *Use after lesson 11, line 3*

Quick   Clap the rhythm while counting out loud, then play the exercise.

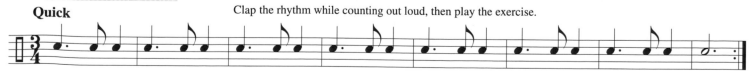

Play the rhythm on all instruments.

30

Extra Credit Exercises

Keyboard Percussion

1. *Use after lesson 1, line 8*

2. *Use after lesson 3, line 5*

3. *Use after lesson 4, line 8*

4. *Use after lesson 5, line 6*

5. *Use after lesson 7, line 5*

6. *Use after lesson 8, line 7*

7. *Use after lesson 10, line 4*

8. *Use after lesson 11, line 3*

Quick

Clap the rhythm while counting out loud, then play the exercise.

PARTS OF A SNARE DRUM

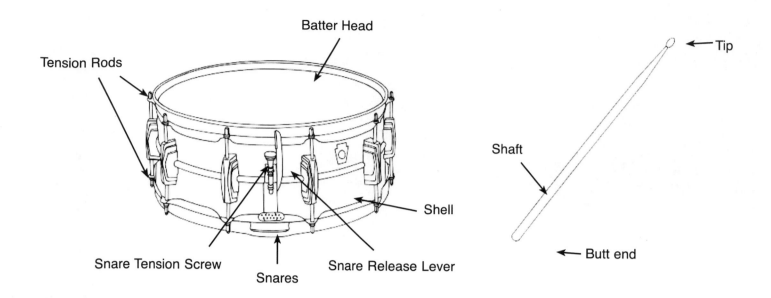

Batter Head

Tip

Tension Rods

Shaft

Shell

Butt end

Snare Tension Screw

Snares

Snare Release Lever

Snare Drum Rudiments Learned in This Book

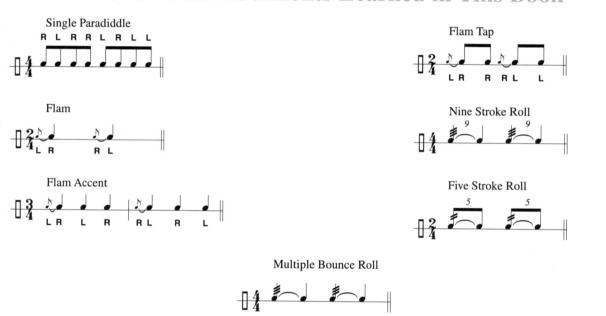

Single Paradiddle

R L R R L R L L

Flam Tap

L R   R R L   L

Flam

L R   R L

Nine Stroke Roll

Flam Accent

L R   L   R   R L   R   L

Five Stroke Roll

Multiple Bounce Roll

Other Techniques and Accessory Instruments Learned

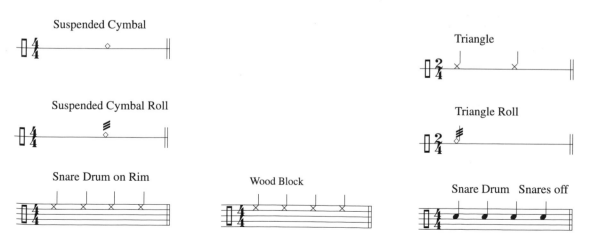

Suspended Cymbal

Triangle

Suspended Cymbal Roll

Triangle Roll

Snare Drum on Rim

Wood Block

Snare Drum   Snares off

RANGE OF KEYBOARD PERCUSSION INSTRUMENTS

Notes Learned in Level 1

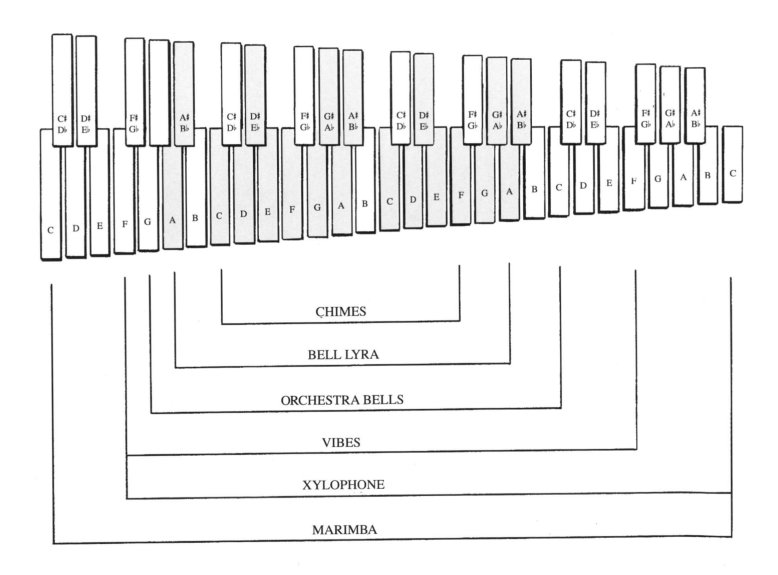

NOTES